THE BOOK OF THE
SCOTTISH GARDEN

A Royal Botanic Garden Edinburgh book

THE BOOK OF THE
SCOTTISH GARDEN

Photographs by Brinsley Burbidge

Text by Fay Young

CANONGATE

First published in Great Britain in 1989 by Moubray House Publishing Ltd. Edinburgh. This edition first published in 1991 by Canongate Books, Edinburgh. Reprinted in 1997.

Photographs © Royal Botanic Garden Edinburgh.
Text © Fay Young 1989

All rights reserved. No part of this book may be reproduced or utilised in any form or by any means electronic or mechanical, including photocopying, recording or by any information storage and retrieval system without prior permission in writing from the Publishers

A CIP catalogue record for this book is available upon request from the British Library

ISBN 0 86241 367 2

Designed by Dorothy Steedman
Typeset in Fenice by Page Phototypesetting Ltd, Edinburgh
Printed in China by Imago Publishing Ltd

On behalf of Brinsley Burbidge and the Royal Botanic Garden Edinburgh we should like to thank all those owners and their agents who allowed access to their properties for the purpose of the photographic survey and, more particularly in this instance, those whose gardens are illustrated in this publication. The latter are H.M. Queen Elizabeth the Queen Mother; His Excellency Mahdi Al-Tajir; The Earl and Countess of Ancram; The Duke of Atholl; Major and Mrs Baxter; Buccleuch Estates Ltd; Cairndow Estates; The Earl and Countess of Cawdor; Crarae Gardens Charitable Trust; Captain N E F Dalrymple-Hamilton; Mrs J B Findlay; Mr & Mrs J R Findlay; City of Glasgow District Council; Mr & Mrs J O Graham; The Grimsthorpe and Drummond Castle Trust; The Earl of Haddington; Historic Buildings and Monuments Directorate (Scottish Development Department); Mr Christopher James; Mr Andrew Kennedy; The Kildrummy Castle Garden Trust; Mr D W N Landale; Mr J & Mrs W Mattingley; Lady Strange and Captain Drummond of Megginch; Sir David Montgomery Bt; The National Trust for Scotland; N E Fife District Council; The Earl and Countess of Perth; Mrs F Raven; Mrs M A Richard; Mr A Roger; Mr N Roger; The Proprietors of Saltoun Hall; The Scottish Wildlife Trust; Mr L Seymour; The Stanley Smith Horticultural Trust; Strathmore Estates (Holding) Ltd; The Earl of Strathmore and Kinghorne; The Duke of Sutherland; The Sutherland Trust; Sir George Taylor VMH; Mr & Mrs Murray Threipland; The University of Dundee.

Fay Young wishes to acknowledge the help and hospitality given to her during the preparation of the text, particularly that of Sir Ilay Campbell, Mrs Jaquetta James, Mrs Lorraine Baxter, Mr Arthur Hall, Mr John Mattingley and The National Trust for Scotland representatives at Kellie Castle and Falkland Palace. She also wishes to thank Mr Alf Evans whose time, patience and endless knowledge were invaluable during her researches into the accurate naming and background history of the plants. The following are also thanked for their help: Ms D Brunton, Dr D F Chamberlain, Dr B J Coppins, Dr J Cullen, Dr C N Page and Mr C Will and his Library staff (all of the Royal Botanic Garden Edinburgh), Sir George Taylor (The Stanley Smith Horticultural Trust) and Mr Eric Robson (The National Trust for Scotland).

The preparation of this book would not have been possible without the enthusiastic commitment of Alan Bennell (Head of Public Services) and Norma Gregory (Publications Officer), both of the Royal Botanic Garden Edinburgh, whose collaboration with the publisher, photographer and text author is gratefully acknowledged. The idea for the book was in part stimulated by an exhibition 'Gardens of Scotland', featuring photographs by Brinsley Burbidge, produced by Paul Nesbitt and Henry Noltie at the Botanic Garden in 1987. The exacting eye of the Marquess of Lansdowne, cast over the material for this publication in its early stages, helped to concentrate our minds wonderfully. We are grateful to Dr Miles Oglethorpe for providing the map of Scotland.

CONTENTS

Foreword by Sir Peter Hutchison

– 7 –

Introduction

– 8 –

Gardens in the Landscape

– 12 –

Wild, Woodland and Water Gardens

– 30 –

House and Garden

– 66 –

The Plantsman's Garden

– 126 –

Map of Scottish Gardens

– 164 –

List of Gardens and Index

– 165 –

The Royal Botanic Garden Edinburgh is Scotland's national Botanic Garden, and has been concerned with the collection and study of plants from all parts of the world for over 300 years. As a source of innumerable new introductions, and authoritative information on their identity, status and cultivation, it has played a seminal role in the development of the Scottish Garden.

It is therefore very appropriate for the Garden to celebrate the wealth and diversity of this important element of our national heritage in this book.

While at Edinburgh Brinsley Burbidge compiled a unique photographic record of many of Scotland's finest gardens, each captured in a series of personal and evocative images. We hope that this book will encourage the reader to explore not just the gardens portrayed in this volume that are open to the public, but also to discover the special qualities of the great variety of others, many of which are accessible thanks to Scotland's Gardens Scheme.

All gardens are ephemeral in nature. Without constant labour and expenditure they will decay. It is only the commitment of many owners and the work of such bodies as the National Council for the Conservation of Plants and Gardens and The National Trust for Scotland that will ensure that our unique garden heritage is protected for future generations.

As Chairman of the Board of Trustees responsible for the work of our national Botanic Garden it is a special pleasure to commend to you this book which is in essence a tribute to the generations of explorers, plantsmen, gardeners and owners whose dedication first created and now sustains the Scottish Garden.

Sir Peter Hutchison, Bt.
Chairman of the Board of Trustees
Royal Botanic Garden Edinburgh

INTRODUCTION

Every autumn for over twenty years F.R.S. Balfour planted a ton of daffodils in the woodland gardens at Dawyck. Creating a garden is a generous pursuit which has as much to do with dreams of the future as it has with digging in the present. Lady Rachel Drummond scattered flower seeds in Stobhall plantation. Walter Murray Guthrie shipped Italian statues from a garden in Padua to decorate the terraces at Torosay.

To explore the gardens of Scotland is to follow a fascinating trail full of surprises left by personalities of the past and constantly added to by new owners and gardeners. If you look very hard you might catch a glimpse of the statues as the ferry approaches Torosay on the Isle of Mull – now that they have been cleaned they stand out strikingly against the surrounding greenery. It is odd to see them there. Just as odd and exciting as the cabbage palms and tree ferns at Logan just south of Stranraer, or the Bonsai collection of perfectly dwarfed Japanese forest trees growing at Dundonnell in the shelter of an old walled garden on the barren coast of Wester Ross, or the warm, friendly kitchen garden full of lavender and roses hidden behind the deceptively dour face of a fortified house.

They all have something in common. The statues; the eucalyptus trees waving in the wind by the water's edge on Mull; the rhododendrons in the gorge overlooking Loch Fyne; the romantic bowers in walled gardens; the Dawyck daffodils which welcome visitors every spring: they are all monuments to the very odd enduring partnership between the gardener and nature which thrives equally on fantasy and hard labour.

Coming relatively late to gardening (the earliest known garden plans date back to the sixteenth and seventeenth centuries) Scotland made up for lost time by producing some of the world's most influential gardeners, botanists and plant collectors. 'To a people of a plodding turn of mind and firm structure of body' noted the 1813 report of the Caledonian Horticultural Society, 'gardening would soon become a very desirable employment.' The report describes gardeners who spent their days digging and their evenings on geometry, drawing and botany. Inspired by the 'unsettled' climate they made the most of short summers

The bridge at Crarae Glen in early autumn.

INTRODUCTION

in walled gardens skilfully designed to trap the sun's warmth (ideal settings for Sir Robert Lorimer's later idealistic interpretation of the kitchen garden full of secret places).

'Plodding personalities' perhaps, but the Scots produced strokes of brilliance. Plant collectors spread abroad and their discoveries fired the imagination of gardeners back home. The result is a remarkably rich variety of great gardens which not only survive but continue to grow despite enormous financial burdens. At Torosay Jaquetta James is developing a new wild garden on the slope beneath the statues and John Mattingley subscribes to newly-gathered Asiatic primulas, expanding the collection begun by his father-in-law Bobby Masterton at Cluny. The future of Scotland's gardens depends on present-day imagination and investment and simply visiting established gardens provides one of the great sources of inspiration. Stately trees and avenues mark the aspirations and physical boundaries of Scottish gardens but within the woodland plantations, the walled garden, and the formal designs around the house you will find that almost anything is possible. 'Visitors enter the (Scottish) garden with raised expectations,' said the 1813 report, 'they very seldom retire disappointed.'

Behind the scenes. Order and cleanliness – characteristic qualities of the Scottish garden – in Carnell potting shed.

Stones and plants blend at Torosay Castle, monuments to the whims and hard work of gardeners past and present.

GARDENS IN THE LANDSCAPE

Each great garden has its own way of fitting in with the wild world around it, borrowing from the landscape, repaying with enhanced scenery. The gardens of Kinross House stretch in a long straight line to take in the ruined castle on Loch Leven and the hills beyond. Dunrobin Castle prefers to block out the Moray Firth: symmetrically ordered flower beds roll down to the water's edge but trees shut out wind and wild scenery. In a sense the gardens of Achamore House begin on the ferry over to the Isle of Gigha. The trees can be seen from the sea, the only woodland in a rocky landscape, but they conceal the real garden of flowering shrubs and you have to climb above their shelter to see across to the Mull of Kintyre or out to Islay, Jura and the Atlantic Ocean. Where a garden begins and ends depends partly on geography and partly on the intentions of its creator.

Over the last three hundred years or more Scottish gardens have developed a fascinating variety of styles in response to the enormous challenge of the natural scenery. How do you landscape mountainsides or cultivate barren coastlines? How do you soften the surroundings of castles and fortified houses which were built quite deliberately in unapproachable places to deter unwelcome visitors? There are basically three simple answers: a garden may borrow from the view, blend in with it or ignore it completely. How and what it grows depends on winds, rain, sun, soil and the lie of the land. The shelter provided by garden trees in turn affects the local climate; shrubs naturalise and spread into the surrounding countryside and neatly drawn boundaries begin to blur.

The first gardens which emerged in the sixteenth and seventeenth centuries tended to disregard the views around them. The parterres of Dunrobin and Drummond first laid out in the early 1600s (and recreated in the nineteenth century) symbolise a private, inward looking world of harmony, order and privilege. Parterres, literally level spaces laid out with flower beds in intricate patterns imitating the French and Italian style of gardening, often displayed a family coat of arms. Dunrobin, a 'house well seated upon a mote hard by the sea,' was seen by the seventeenth century historian, Sir Richard Gordon, in a 'pleasant garden planted with all kinds of froots, hearbs and floors used in this kingdom'. Twentieth century visitors may

Looking west: the view from the highest point of Achamore House Gardens on the Isle of Gigha.

catch a glimpse of the baronial turrets from the main road but the gardens are best appreciated from the castle itself. Drummond Castle lies behind neatly managed parkland with avenues of beech trees which suggest that something important lies beyond. But nothing prepares the visitor for the sudden sight of the thirteen acre parterre on hanging terraces which seem to have been dropped far below the castle. The extraordinarily compelling pattern of topiary and flower beds, based on the saltire, takes no more notice of the Ochils in the background than it does of the natural contours and bumps of the ground itself.

To Percy Cane, however, 'some of the loveliest things in the garden', came from an appreciation of the possibilities offered by 'skilful management of the contours of the ground'. In redesigning the gardens of Monteviot House two decades or so ago, Cane sought the 'harmonious relation of garden to house and garden to surrounding scenery'. He changed the level and slope of the terrace gardens to keep an uninterrupted view of the River Teviot. Similarly the Japanese Gardens at Torosay Castle on Mull 'borrow' a view of neighbouring Castle Duart and look up to Loch Linnhe. Three hundred years earlier Sir William Bruce, well ahead of his time, had also made use of natural props in the axial designs for his houses and gardens. Just as he lined Balcaskie up with the Bass Rock, he designed the central axis of Kinross in 1675 to focus on the ruin of Loch Leven Castle, thereby uniting the symmetrically formal garden with its natural setting. Daniel Defoe considered Kinross House to be 'the most beautiful and regular piece of architecture in all Scotland'.

The wilderness does not always offer a sheltered setting with a conveniently placed rock or ruin to close a vista. 'Let the mountains be covered with wood and the water shaded by trees', urged John Claudius Loudon, 'the scene is instantly changed: what was before cold and barren is now rich, noble and full of variety.' Loudon, the prolific nineteenth century gardening writer, was preaching what earlier improving landowners had already started to practise. The imposing view offered of Blair Castle to motorists on the A9 depends on the huge conifer plantations undertaken by the 4th Duke of Atholl between 1774 and 1830. He created a setting which both blends with and dominates the surrounding scenery – and at the same time he pioneered the commercial reforestation of Scottish hills. By the time the seeds of plants newly discovered on the other side of the world began to flood into Scotland there were woodlands to offer them shelter.

Ultimately a successful garden builds upon the natural resources of its setting. The contrast between the warm, wet west and the cold, dry east is fully exploited by the Royal

Botanic Garden Edinburgh with its outstations of Dawyck, Benmore and Logan conveniently located to offer a range of growing conditions to plants collected from all over the world. In Edinburgh tender plants need protection in glasshouses while at Logan, warmed by the Gulf Stream, tree ferns and cabbage palms grow out of doors giving a strangely subtropical look to the south west tip of Scotland. Logan was a traditional Scottish walled garden growing flowers and vegetables side by side until the middle of the last century when Kenneth and Douglas McDouall began to collect plants from the warm temperate regions of the world. They were typical of the hardy breed of pioneer gardeners and botanists who have influenced the shape of gardens over the last 200 years. Many of them fulfilled their botanical ambitions abroad but some like Osgood Mackenzie stayed at home to create what has become perhaps the most characteristic kind of Scottish garden. In 1862 Mackenzie began to cultivate the bare red sandstone rock of Inverewe in Wester Ross: first came deer and rabbit fences, next the scots and corsican pines, next creel loads of soil – a painstakingly slow process, but it brought about a garden which now attracts thousands of visitors every year. Inverewe, like the wild gardens of Achamore, Ardtornish and Crarae, has given new life and colour to its natural landscape setting.

The landscape of the Teviot valley shapes Monteviot garden.

GARDENS IN THE LANDSCAPE

Borrowed views. **Above:** *Torosay in its woodland setting seen from Castle Duart on the Island of Mull.* **Opposite above:** *the formal garden framed by gates to the wild garden.* **Opposite below:** *Castle Duart in return provides a focal point for the view from Torosay's Japanese Garden.*

GARDENS IN THE LANDSCAPE

Rocky masses, streams and meadows dictated the character of the wild garden developed by botanist John Raven on Ardtornish overlooking Loch Aline and Mull. Maintained since his death by his wife Faith, the garden presents a perfect balance between specialist plants and natural setting.

GARDENS IN THE LANDSCAPE

Opposite: a sub-tropical look for what was once a traditional Scottish kitchen garden: Logan exploits the warmth which travels from the Gulf of Mexico to the west of Scotland.
Above left*: the view west from Inverewe garden, with* Celmisia *in the foreground, shows the barren landscape which Osgood Mackenzie transformed into a lush environment by planting trees.* ***Above right****: Chilean firebush and Himalayan blue poppies. Inverewe brings life and colour to its surrounding landscape.*

GARDENS IN THE LANDSCAPE

Percy Cane's design for Monteviot House gardens was deliberately subservient to the River Teviot. Arches through the wall of the river garden create framed 'pictures' of the valley, the gradual slope of the terraces allows uninterrupted views of the river.

Above: looking up the slope of the rose garden.

GARDENS IN THE LANDSCAPE

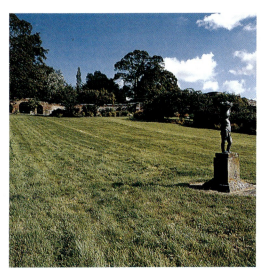

Above left: the herb garden against the background curve of the Teviot.
Above right: a view from the river up to the house. *Below:* steps down to the water.

GARDENS IN THE LANDSCAPE

Above: Stobhall sits high enough to command views of the Tay Valley.
Below: clipped yews in the formal garden and the trees beneath the house are kept low to allow fine views of the river. *Opposite:* Crarae House surrounded by one of the great west coast gardens which exploits a wooded gorge as a foil for the colour and shape of its exotic trees and shrubs.

GARDENS IN THE LANDSCAPE

Above left: Drummond Castle; the grandest surviving formal garden in Scotland, first laid out in 1630 and redesigned in the 1820s and 1830s. An extraordinary exercise in symmetry and order against the background of Perthshire farmland. *Above right*: the view back to the house from the 'natural' parkland. The pond was made in 1800 during improvements to the grounds, the bridge carrying the picturesque drive was built for Queen Victoria's visit in 1842.
Opposite: order and romance: an eyecatching vista leads out to the wider landscape.

GARDENS IN THE LANDSCAPE

Opposite above: Sir William Bruce designed Kinross House and gardens in the 1680s, drawing the main axis to align, through the Fish Gate, with the ruined Castle of Loch Leven (one time prison of Mary Queen of Scots). The linking of a formal garden with its natural setting was unusual at that time.
Opposite left: a view of Aberdeenshire's agricultural landscape from the walled enclosure of Crathes Castle. *Opposite right:* sheltered from the east winds and a view of the Moray Firth, the elegant symmetry of a seventeenth century parterre revived in the 1840s at Dunrobin Castle (probably by Sir Charles Barry, architect of the Houses of Parliament).

Below: Blair Castle, in the woodland setting created by the 4th Duke of Atholl in the late eighteenth century, perfectly unites the house with the Perthshire landscape.

WILD, WOODLAND AND WATER GARDENS

Wild gardens have a delicate relationship with nature. At Crarae rhododendrons spread freely down the steep slopes of a natural gorge among conifers and eucalyptus trees. They blend beautifully with the mountains overlooking Loch Fyne but they are there only because of inspired and energetic interference with the surrounding wilderness. Left to its own devices, nature makes a haphazard job of covering rock faces and glens. Across the wall at the top of the hill you can see what would grow naturally in the gorge: a dense cover of scrub oak, birch and bracken always threatening to reclaim its territory.

Part of the excitement of Scotland's wild gardens comes from the pioneering spirit which created them. Explorers sought new plants in foreign wildernesses, bold gardeners grew them in equally untamed ground back home. In the 1920s while George Forrest was climbing thousands of feet in the Himalayas to discover rhododendrons and primulas, Sir George Campbell was making his way carefully down the glen at Crarae, compost in one jacket pocket and some newly introduced young plants in the other, to set them out in a cleared space as nature might have done.

Crarae Glen, now run by a charitable trust, was Sir George's creation but his mother Grace Campbell had redesigned the gardens round the house to take new alpines, dwarf conifers and rhododendrons discovered by her nephew, Reginald Farrer the plant collector, in 1914. During the next twenty years new discoveries were to change the look of Scottish gardens. Rhododendrons and other exotic flowering shrubs invaded the woodlands of established gardens such as Brodick, Dawyck, Inverewe and Keir and later helped create others like Achamore on the Isle of Gigha. Sir George did not directly subscribe to the Far Eastern expeditions of Farrer, Forrest, and Kingdon Ward but others did and they exchanged seeds among themselves. Crarae grows gifts from Dawyck, Gigha, Inverewe, and the Royal Botanic Garden Edinburgh which became the world authority on rhododendrons.

But spring and autumn flowering shrubs occupy only one level of the woodland garden. First of all came trees: twentieth century gardens depend on a nineteenth century canopy of trees to provide shelter from biting salty winds and filter the heavy rain which in places on

*Spring flowering rhododendrons in the natural gorge
at the centre of Crarae Glen garden.*

the west coast varies from seventy to one hundred inches a year. It is hard to believe that when Samuel Johnson travelled to the Hebrides in 1773 he saw only the gloom of desolation and 'to give nature a more cheerful face' he suggested planting trees. 'To drop seeds into the ground requires little labour and no skill.' As it happened, the 'Planting Duke' of Atholl in Perthshire was about to pioneer wide-scale planting of commercial woodland restoring forested areas destroyed by centuries of misuse: between 1774 and 1830 he planted fourteen million larch. By the 1830s David Douglas was sending back from western North America seeds of sitka spruce, lodgepole pine and Douglas fir. Trees were planted in millions on Scottish hills and gardening landowners took pride in growing rare specimens for their own sake.

To 'drop seeds' collected from the other side of the world into barely cultivated land required an act of faith, imagination and – since trees may not reach maturity for forty years – great patience. Osgood Mackenzie, who in 1862 began to create Inverewe out of barren rock, had to wait fifteen years for the scots and corsican pines to provide shelter for more tender shrubs and plants and he 'confessed' that foreign trees were hardier than Scottish natives. When Pearce Patrick planted the famous avenue of Wellingtonias at Benmore in 1865 he had no idea what would happen. *Sequoiadendron giganteum* had entered the country less than ten years earlier so (as an old photograph now missing showed) he took the precaution of planting silver firs between each tree for the first twenty years. The size of the 'Big Trees' now shows the effect of heavy rain, warm air and long hours of summer daylight. Sir George also began with trees, specialising in rare conifers such as Korean pines and silver firs, which he planted as he cleared the scrub, little by little, each year.

Wild gardens which exploit beautiful places with exotic plants inspire romantic notions of follies and fantasies among the trees. In nineteenth century novels heroines often wander astray in the woodland plantations. Barncluith in Lanarkshire now suggests the decadent romance of a cultivated place giving itself up to the wild. But even one hundred years ago the flowers hidden among the wooded gorge on the River Avon moved Sir Robert Lorimer. 'In the twilight or the moonlight destinies might be determined in this garden.'

However, there is little room for sentiment in the day to day management of the woodland garden. Imitating nature requires a sensitive eye, a sharp blade and good ditches to cope with the rain which will wash away paths and drown plants. Given a chance nature will overwhelm the ground floor of spring bulbs, lilies, and delicate ferns with the native dense scrub of trees and bracken and rogue naturalising rhododendrons. A dominant weed in woodland gardens, *Rhododendron ponticum* was introduced 200 years ago as game cover and allowed to spread because of its pretty pinkish mauve flowers. To develop the higher slopes at Benmore with rare Himalayan species of rhododendron, the ponticum must be hacked back. Not even trees are indispensable. Each woodland gardener notes with sorrow a tree destroyed by a gale but almost immediately sees the benefit of the new space opening up a view, allowing room for a new plant. Arthur Hall, assistant curator at Benmore, removes trees which are dangerous, diseased or blocking the view: 'a beautiful tree is no use if there is no room to see it.' In building up a scientific collection of rare and valuable trees he is careful to avoid a plantation full of trees of the same age which are vulnerable to mass destruction when a gale blows.

Crarae has been likened to a Himalayan ravine. On a misty day part of Benmore, where Japanese pines cling to bare rock cliff, looks like a Japanese painting. The skilful handling of the wild garden is an art which can produce surprises. Since the strimmer was introduced to cut back invading weeds at Crarae wild flowers – anemones, primroses and wild strawberries – have covered the ground, seeding themselves in the mulch left behind. Other plants such as *Rhododendron wardii* with its cream flowers, *Rhododendron lacteum*, and tree-like specimens of *Rhododendron macabeanum* full of globular yellow trusses have been left to seed in many places resulting in rhododendron hybrids much to the delight of Crarae and the occasional concern of purists. 'This place is full of hybrids,' one visitor said, 'including the dogs.'

Autumn. Maple in the woodland garden at Keir.

WILD, WOODLAND AND WATER GARDENS

Below left: view to Holy Loch overlooking the formal garden at Benmore showing garden conifers against a forest background.
Below centre: the Wellingtonia avenue planted between 1865 and 1870. The tallest tree is more than 140 feet tall and still growing.
Below right: autumn colour among the conifers. Open spaces show trees to best advantage.

Opposite: Pinus sylvestris *(scots pine) the oldest trees in the gardens planted in 1820, the first extensive planting of the Cowal peninsula.*

WILD, WOODLAND AND WATER GARDENS

Opposite: Cercidiphyllum *among the water plants on the River Eachaig running through the Younger Botanic Garden at Benmore.*

Above left: Aleuria aurantia, *the 'orange peel' fungus found in woodland.*
Above right: *autumn view of the pond area.* **Below left:** *cones of* Cupressocyparis.
Below right: *a carpet of the moss* Polytrichum commune *found in damp areas.*

— WILD, WOODLAND AND WATER GARDENS —

Above left: colour at Crarae in spring and,
above right, more dramatically in autumn Disanthus *against a background of conifers.*
Opposite: spring flowering rhododendrons from the Himalayas grow happily
in a Highland gorge.

WILD, WOODLAND AND WATER GARDENS

Opposite: candelabra primulas among the trees looking down to Loch Fyne from Crarae.
Above left: Viburnum *'Crarae'*. *Above right*: autumn at Crarae.

WILD, WOODLAND AND WATER GARDENS

*Opposite: conifers provide a dark contrast to autumn colour in the formal terraces at Keir.
Above: spring. Looking across a meadow of narcissi to Keir woodland garden
begun in 1850 and stocked earlier this century with shrubs and plants from
the Kingdon Ward collection.*

WILD, WOODLAND AND WATER GARDENS

Woodland walks connect formal and wild gardens at Keir and lead through the shrubbery to the Yew House, formed from clipped yew.

WILD, WOODLAND AND WATER GARDENS

Opposite: autumn leaves in a stream at Dawyck. Scotland is well supplied with
natural lochs and rivers which provide a peaceful setting for water-loving plants.
Above: 'natural' water gardens can be man-made. The Hen Poo at Duns Castle was created
in the early nineteenth century from a straight-sided eighteenth century canal.

WILD, WOODLAND AND WATER GARDENS

Above left : Kildrummy water garden, created in 1900 by a firm of Japanese landscape gardeners, follows the path of a stream dammed to create lakes.
Above right: reflections in the Japanese water garden at Stobo. **Opposite:** *Stobo makes the most of a series of waterfalls looking up to a focal point of the bridge.*

WILD, WOODLAND AND WATER GARDENS

Opposite: the stream running through Bargany woodland garden
created for rhododendrons by Sir North Dalrymple-Hamilton in the 1920s.
Above: plants for reflection around Inverewe pond.
Following pages: Crarae in autumn.

WILD, WOODLAND AND WATER GARDENS

Above: Rodgersia *in the foreground of the pond at Dundee University Botanic Garden.*
Below: Mimulus, *the monkey flower, grows at the water's edge in St Andrews Botanic Garden.*

WILD, WOODLAND AND WATER GARDENS

Above: falls leading to Keir water garden.
Below: a richly planted pond at Dundonnell replaced a weed-infested rockery.

WILD, WOODLAND AND WATER GARDENS

The formality of the old established garden at Brodick Castle merges with the wilder woodland garden planned by the Duchess of Montrose in the 1920s to display rhododendrons discovered by Scottish plant collectors.

WILD, WOODLAND AND WATER GARDENS

Above: azalea with lichen at Keir.
Opposite: azalea terrace at Dawyck.

WILD, WOODLAND AND WATER GARDENS

*Three storeys of the woodland garden – bluebells, rhododendrons and conifers –
at Strone with Loch Fyne in the background.*

WILD, WOODLAND AND WATER GARDENS

Crarae

WILD, WOODLAND AND WATER GARDENS

Rhododendrons helped to inspire the creation of Scotland's wild gardens and provide raw material for the continuing development of decorative hybrids for the border and glasshouse. **Above left:** *Rhododendron loderi 'Joseph Hooker' growing in the shrub and woodland gardens of Achamore House and seen in close up* **below right.** *The other plants shown here display a selection from the Royal Botanic Garden Edinburgh.*
Above right: Rhododendron citriniflorum var. horaeum.
Below left: Rhododendron calophytum.

Above left: Rhododendron oldhamii, *an evergreen azalea.*
Above right: Rhododendron sulfureum. *Below left:* Rhododendron javanicum.
Below right: Rhododendron jasminiflorum.

WILD, WOODLAND AND WATER GARDENS

'Such an atmosphere about the place', said Lorimer almost a hundred years ago, 'Destinies might be determined in this garden.' The wilderness is reclaiming Barncluith but even decay has beauty. The clear outlines of the remains of the formal terraces show the garden could still be saved.

HOUSE AND GARDEN

Like 'the sun sending forth its beams' all walks, trees and hedges must radiate from the house, wrote John Reid in the *Scots Gardener* of 1683. The house was to be the centre of a symmetrically planned scheme: 'as the sun is centre of this world, and the nose the centre of the face, . . . and as it is unseemly to see a man . . . his nose standing at one side the face . . .' trees would be planted to allow perfect perspective from the front door; fruit, flowers and vegetables would be arranged in geometrically precise plots bordered with lavender, thyme, hyssop or rue and where each neat box-lined path met would be a tree trimmed to a sphere or pyramid.

It sounds a little rigid but nature refuses to stick to geometry for long and by midsummer the straight lines are softened with a haze of blue and pink flowers. You can still see gardens laid out very much as Reid ordered 300 years ago thanks partly to the Victorians who set about restoring some of the formal designs swept away by the improving landscapers of the eighteenth century. The kitchen garden, meanwhile, had survived as a characteristically Scottish design to make the most of a short growing season. Behind the sometimes daunting walls of Scotland's fortified houses lie warmly sheltered kitchen gardens where espalier apples and pears grow beside honeysuckle and roses. Some of the larger country houses keep their walled garden at a distance and look on to ornamental terraces while others open straight into a walled garden. 'Just a house and a garden,' wrote Sir Robert Lorimer 'but what a paradise can such a place be made.' Secret places in a walled garden appealed to late nineteenth century idealists like Lorimer who restored the gardens of Kellie and Earlshall to suit the spirit of the house, creating surprises of 'gardens within gardens' and even plants within plants as climbing roses scrambled through spring flowering fruit trees. Today enthusiasts continue to restore, maintain and develop the gardens laid out by earlier generations (allowing for the limitations imposed by tending perhaps eleven fully planted acres with two or three gardeners instead of eight) with the same sensitive attention

Cawdor Castle: lavender outlines the rose beds as recommended by John Reid in 1683 for edging borders in the kitchen garden.

Curved walls provide a sheltered enclosure for herbaceous borders and climbing plants in the river garden at Monteviot.

to detail: the head gardener at Kellie prefers to clip the box hedging by hand, believing the noise of machinery to be out of place.

Gardening is a compulsive occupation which leaves lots of room for contradictions. While rhododendrons and spring flowers are left to roam freely in woodland plantations, nature is kept in tight check near the house, defying the untidy mess of the world outside. The formal garden is an extension of the house – in 1786 Lady Rachel Drummond called the parterre at Stobhall her garden withdrawing room where she took dinner guests to sit among scented roses in box-edged compartments.

Topiary, revived by the Victorians, defines a territorial line in often defensive shapes (battlements, buttresses, sentinels). Lorimer complemented the turreted shapes of Earlshall with an extraordinary arrangement of old yews rising straight out of the lawn, an army of chessmen marking the shape of the saltire. Percy Cane, using a seventeenth century engraving as a guide for his design of Falkland Palace garden in 1946, outlined the old ruined

Torosay Castle, Isle of Mull: walls of the old kitchen garden at the foot of a terraced garden laid out by Sir Robert Lorimer at the turn of the century.

castle walls with columnar *Chamaecyparis lawsoniana,* echoing the shapes with a long bed of lupins underneath. 'The architectural character of any house must be the keynote for any architectural treatment in the garden,' he wrote, 'but it is a keynote on which an infinite number of variations may be played.'

Parterres – as recreated in the 1950s at Pitmedden to a seventeenth century design with three miles of box hedge and 40,000 bedding plants – are laid out to mark ownership in a family crest or intricate ornamental pattern best seen from the windows above. In the architectural framework of the 'outdoors room' plants are treated like sculpture and the living texture is punctuated by stone statues, monuments and sundials, gathering moss as they make focal points on walks around the garden.

Even the lively growth of a herbaceous border is laid out to a carefully drawn plan; the apparently artless informal tumble of old-fashioned flowers within a strictly formal setting was pioneered by Lorimer. Reid had worked to a restricted 'pallette' of carnations, tulips, cranesbills and sow breads. From the turn of the twentieth century a bewildering choice of exotic shrubs, bulbs and herbaceous plants began to flood into the country offering potential for a completely different kind of gardening but in the borders round the house they still usually submitted to the rule of the designing hand. At Crathes Castle from 1926 Sir James Burnett of Leys collected rare plants and his wife Sybil arranged them in borders for colour and contrast.

There is rarely a clear division between the purely ornamental and the simply functional in Scottish gardens. The walls, works of art in themselves, are there because they are needed to trap the sun in a cold and unreliable climate. 'Hot' walls were lined with twisting charcoal-fired flues to ripen tender fruit. Lean-to peach houses took the control of nature a step further and, with the introduction of cast-iron and steam-heating, gardens were adorned with palatial glass buildings to grow the exotic fruit and plants which were brought home from abroad. By the mid nineteenth century the Buccleuch estate at Dalkeith, boasting one of the grandest conservatories in the country, was typical of a large number of country households able to choose from an astonishing variety of fresh fruit: peaches, nectarines, grapes, figs, melons, pineapples.

The Dalkeith conservatory is just an empty frame now, the ornamental gardens around it disappeared long ago. A garden is a very unruly work of art always trying to grow out of its framework. Lorimer's hollyhocks at Kellie have succumbed to a fungus just as Cane's beds at Falkland have become sick of lupins and the tall cypress trees vital to his plan have had to be replaced with a new more compact form to allow visitors freedom of movement. Plants outgrow the best-laid schemes but historic gardens still flourish and dedicated gardeners and owners have to balance the needs and economics of the present with the designs of the past. In 1983, ninety years after Lorimer restored Earlshall the new owners found yews and lawns unkempt and overgrown and, worse than that, the herbaceous borders had been 'poisoned' with weed killer. With care and understanding plants have been restored and replaced and visitors may still see Lorimer's 'borders of brightest flowers backed up by low espaliers hanging with shining apples'. The biggest alteration planned is to restock some of the vegetable plots with less labour-intensive herbs for the house. Neither Reid nor Lorimer would be likely to disagree with that.

Symmetrical enough to satisfy John Reid: a walk from Malleny house leads to a circular pool between two clipped yews.

HOUSE AND GARDEN

Opposite: *Cane's design for Falkland gardens used a repetition of vertical lines to echo the shape of the palace.* ***Above:*** *old fashioned plants chosen for colourful effect with netting used to keep them in place; lemon-yellow lady's mantle terminates the view at the end of the herbaceous border.*
Below left: *tall Lawson's cypress trees outline the original fifteenth century castle wall, now replaced with a more compact hybrid form to give visitors room to walk along the terrace.*
Below right: *a form of* Nepeta *runs along the wall, softening the straight line.*

Above: Ladybird Poppies in the island bed.
Below: a less formal view of Falkland Palace from the island beds in the lawn.

Below: Nepeta *in bloom at Kellie Castle, the Lorimer family home.*

Lorimer's plan for the kitchen garden at Kellie Castle is carefully maintained today, much as he drew it in 1888 at the age of twenty four.
Four main compartments are divided by hedges and walks and there are two separate 'secret' corner gardens. Fruit and vegetables grow among flowers as they did in Reid's day, in keeping with the age of the house. Lorimer's use of old-fashioned cottage garden plants (illustrated in the next two pages) was recorded by Gertrude Jekyll and influenced many garden designs.

Above left: pink paeonies, a cottage garden favourite, at Kellie.
Above right: Penstemon *and* Erigeron *in the border backed by a Peace rose framing the seat by Sir Robert's son the sculptor Hew Lorimer.*
Below left: walk lined by versicolour roses leads to a sundial at the central point.
Below right: roses and sweet william chosen for aromatic scent.
Opposite: hand-clipped box- lined borders showing Inula *and white paeonies in the foreground.*

Earlshall, Fife. **Opposite:** *Lorimer restored Earlshall and its gardens between 1891 and 1900. Like Kellie, Earlshall opens directly into the sheltered enclosure of the castle walls, to Lorimer the ideal garden setting.*
Above: *vistas and 'intersecting walks of shaven grass' connecting different compartments within the garden: Lorimer's design influenced many great twentieth century gardens including Crathes and Hidcote.*
Below left: *view from the paved garden to the focal point of a Lorimer seat.*
Below right: *warm shelter for a carpeting of dwarf and spreading plants.*

Above: Philadelphus *and* Rosa rubrifolia *in a decorative corner of the mixed border at Malleny.* ***Below:*** *hostas in bloom at Malleny.* ***Opposite:*** *astilbes, chrysanthemums and clipped evergreen shrubs in a group of beds at Megginch.*

HOUSE AND GARDEN

Decorative buildings began with a practical purpose. Doocots were built from the thirteenth century to provide a source of fresh meat in winter as a break from the salted meat of cattle killed at the end of summer. In 1503 James IV ordered all lords and lairds to make deer parks, fish ponds and doocots for the community. After the introduction of turnips from Sweden as winter cattle feed redundant doocots became a picturesque focal point for gardens.

Opposite: Megginch doocot built in 1806 by Captain Robert Drummond, bears a windvane of his East Indiaman, the General Elliot. **Above left:** early nineteenth century doocot at Crathes rebuilt in 1935. **Above right:** Mertoun doocot, dated 1576, is said to be the oldest in Scotland.

HOUSE AND GARDEN

Above and opposite: exotic fruits made their mark on garden architecture. The Pineapple folly gardenhouse at Dunmore, was built in 1761 thirty years after the introduction of pineapples to Scotland. **Below left**: a stone bridge built in 1838 as a feature in the woodland garden at Dawyck.
Below centre: the Garden House at Kellie, topped with a small stone cockerel, was designed by Sir Robert Lorimer.
Below right: a replica of a Chinese moon gate at Leith Hall.

HOUSE AND GARDEN

Above: *woodland folly, Saltoun.*
Opposite above right: *the thatched cottage, a contrast to the formality at Mellerstain House. The other illustrations on this page show the Bavarian summerhouse, one of three follies built at Brodick last century by the 11th Duke of Hamilton for his wife, Princess Mairi of Baden.*

*Conservatories, a triumphant achievement of the industrial revolution,
took the mastering of nature to higher levels of skill and decoration in response to
the challenge of new plants discovered abroad. One of Scotland's grandest and
most ambitious glasshouses was designed and built by William Burn
at Dalkeith Palace in 1832 as a centre for the formal garden.
The twelve-sided building with its doric columns and central chimney
impressed contemporaries such as John Claudius Loudon, who foresaw gigantic greenhouses
covering acres of market gardens and parks.
Now the glass and surrounding gardens have gone.*

*New plant houses built in 1967 extend the range of plants grown at the Royal Botanic Garden Edinburgh. **Above**: in the Cactus House, where plants are arranged geographically, Agave attenuata from America, frames the picture with Dracaena draco, the Canary Islands dragon tree, and the tall stems of Aloe bainesii from South Africa, in the background. **Below**: bromeliads in the landscaped setting of the Temperate Aquatic House. **Opposite**: the Temperate Palm House opened in 1858, still the tallest glasshouse in Britain. Inside, the spectacular palm, Livistona australis, commemorates Patrick Murray, Laird of Livingston, who provided plants for the first Botanic Garden at Holyrood when it was founded in 1670.*

Above: Collection of ancient Japanese bonsai conifers grown in traditional porcelain pots under the protection of lath-houses at Dundonnell in Ross and Cromarty.
Below left: peaches grown in lean-to glasshouses at Drummond, Perthshire with curved panes for efficient drainage. *Below right*: a Victorian planting of tree ferns in Kibble Palace, one of the largest glasshouses in Britain, which was transferred from John Kibble's Loch Long estate to Glasgow Botanic Garden in 1873.
Opposite: Kibble Palace.

HOUSE AND GARDEN

Previous pages*: at Fingask Castle, Perthshire, overlooking the Carse of Gowrie, a group of nineteenth century stone figures play cards in the shelter of a clipped yew.*

Opposite*: the terrace at Fingask looking across the Carse of Gowrie.*
Above left*: a wellhead surrounded by bergenias.* ***Above centre****: stone lions and clipped yews.*
Above right*: the 1562 sundial was originally located at Holyrood Palace.*

HOUSE AND GARDEN

Opposite: fountain and statue at Kinross added in 1902 when the gardens were remade to the original seventeenth century design of Sir William Bruce.
Above left: modern art at Stobhall.
Above right: the Urn at Haddo a nineteenth century memorial in a vista of lime trees.
Below left: the multi-faceted sundial in Pitmedden Great Garden.
Below right: an astrolabe marks the centre at Kellie.

Above: one of the many statues at Torosay Castle brought to Mull from a derelict garden near Padua by Walter Murray Guthrie at the turn of the century to decorate the Italianate terraces laid out by Lorimer.
Opposite: 'Smiler', one of two marble lions giving the name to Torosay's Lion terrace.

HOUSE AND GARDEN

Opposite: Lion terrace beneath the two Lorimer pergolas.
Above left: urns decorate the kitchen garden walls which give shelter to colourful climbers and, *above right and below left,* espalier apples. This one is 'James Grieve'. *Below right:* Lonicera sempervirens.

HOUSE AND GARDEN

*Above left: a bed of antirrhinums sheltered by a wall of Caithness flagstones at the Castle of Mey. **Above right**: beds of roses, tansy and nasturtiums surrounded by local gravel mixed with sea-shells at Mey. **Opposite above**: a view into the walled garden from the fountain outside the west wall at Kailzie. **Opposite below**: blue* Eryngium, *pink* Geranium *and white* Anaphalis *at Kailzie.*

Above: Agapanthus *in front of the 'pavilion' at Logan.* *Opposite:* Aubrieta, Iberis, Alyssum *and grey* Tanacetum *growing on a wall at Keir.*

Opposite: walls of box-hedging at Pitmedden. In Reid's day the compartments would be filled with herbs but modern bedding plants give prolonged colour.
Above: a gate through the garden wall at Earlshall.

HOUSE AND GARDEN

Above: early twentieth century wrought iron decoration, possibly by Lutyens, in the eighteenth century garden wall at Priorwood.
Below: walls retain heat and provide space for bee-boles at Kellie.
Opposite: a work of art in itself, Edzell wall with blue and white Lobelia in the bee-bole holes.

Two views of the spectacular herbaceous border at Carnell, laid out in 1906, and still containing many of the original plants ranging from tall filipendulas to small evening primroses. Organic compost is one of the secrets of success.

Above left: pansies, Galtonia *and* Phlox *in a mixed herbaceous border at Mertoun.*
Above right: *a blue and white border at Malleny;* Campanula lactiflora *with contrasting white roses.*
Below left: *climbing roses and yellow* Cephalaria *in the mixed perennial border at Glamis.*
Below right: *the herbaceous border at Pitmedden, which traditionally lined the walled garden walks, was laid out from 1955 at the same time as the parterre.*
Opposite: *roses, potentillas, and delphiniums dominate Dunrobin's mixed border.*

HOUSE AND GARDEN

*Opposite: traditional well-planted herbaceous border at Cawdor.
Above: planted for contrast; pink* Penstemon *and white galtonias
in Lady Sybil's Aviary border at Crathes. **Below**: the influence of new plants;
Cardiocrinum giganteum (Giant Himalayan Lily) at Logan.*

Above: holly and yew topiary at Fingask.
Opposite: statuary at Drummond in danger of being overtaken by an enormous yew which has long outgrown its shape. Topiary, used to decorate gardens since Roman times, came to Scotland in the fifteenth century via France and Holland and was revived by the Victorians. Yews which may live for more than 1000 years give a sense of permanence to their surroundings: clipped yews define private territory in defensive or even aggressive shapes.

Opposite: topiary marks the boundaries of the terrace garden at Megginch.
The yews were said to be very old in 1700.
Above left: extravagant figures set out at Megginch in the 1890s.
Above right: a gold and green yew crown fashioned at Megginch
to commemorate Queen Victoria's Golden Jubilee in 1887
(and the golden wedding of John and Frances Drummond in 1885).

Above and below: corkscrew chessmen mark the saltire in the central pleasance at Earlshall. Lorimer had them transplanted from a derelict Edinburgh garden in 1894. Lutyens later used a similar planting at Great Dixter, Sussex. *Opposite*: needing a trim. Clipping takes about a month at the end of summer.

Opposite: Pitmedden has a total of three miles of box hedging to be kept in trim.
Above: buttresses of yew at Pitmedden.

THE PLANTSMAN'S GARDEN

Plants from the other side of the world dictate the shape of Cluny House gardens. Paths through the trees change direction from summer to summer according to the movement of Himalayan newcomers such as *Primula bulleyana* and *Primula beesiana* which have made themselves so much at home in Scotland that they compete happily with the robust native bluebell for space in woodland glades and often win.

These are candelabra primulas, the 'plants of everyone' discovered by George Forrest on his first and toughest expedition to south west China from 1904 to 1906. Employed to collect seed for A.K. Bulley of Bees in Liverpool, Forrest was the only survivor of a Tibetan lama attack on a missionary community in the Upper Mekong. Reports of his death were wired back to Sir Isaac Bayley Balfour, Regius Keeper at the Royal Botanic Garden in Edinburgh. But, mourning the loss of specimens, field notes and photographs abandoned in his flight, Forrest turned up not only alive and with an extraordinary batch of surviving seeds but ready to go back for more.

Thanks to Forrest our gardens have been enriched with *Gentiana sino-ornata*, *Nomocharis*, himalayan poppies, *Lilium* and hundreds of primulas and rhododendrons gathered over a total of seventeen years in China. Some need specialist treatment but most grow very well in Scotland and perhaps that is not surprising: a country which provides many gardens with cold, dry winters and cool, wet summers is a good place to sow seed collected from the slopes and valleys of the Himalayas.

There is a fascinating, paradoxical blooming in the flower beds and hothouses of the gardens we visit on Sunday afternoons. Delicate flowers of great beauty are here because of the grim determination and physical violence often endured by explorers to discover and collect them. 'It is only Scots dourness which carries me on', Forrest wrote home after the fifth climb of 4,000 feet to photograph *Primula pinnatifida* with a heavy plate camera, 'for the cultivation of patience . . . I recommend photographing of alpines in Yunnan.'

Royal Botanic Garden Edinburgh. Aristolochia trilobata, *a warm greenhouse climber, native to South America and the West Indies, closely related to the hardy 'Dutchman's Pipe'. Discovered in 1775 and according to the natives said to be a cure for snake bite.*

The important part played by Scottish botanists and gardeners over the last 200 years is recorded quietly on the labels identifying each plant in botanic gardens all over the world: Forrest, Fortune, Douglas, Cox, Menzies, Masson, Balfour, Sherriff and Forsyth. Plants such as flowering currant and winter jasmine which announce the changing seasons in our gardens came from the other sides of the world with the help of brave and eccentric personalities. *Pseudotsuga menziesii* (the Douglas fir) is a memorial to the Perthshire naturalist David Douglas whose travels in North America in the 1820s for Kew provided us with the flowering currant *(Ribes sanguineum)* among many other garden plants. Douglas survived river rapids and whirlpools before meeting a gruesome end in Hawaii where he fell into a pit dug to trap cattle and was gored to death by a bull. *Rhododendron fortunei* pays tribute to Robert Fortune – born in Berwickshire, trained at the Royal Botanic Garden Edinburgh and eventually curator of Chelsea Physic Garden – who survived the dangers of travelling through China in 1843 by wearing Chinese dress, growing a pigtail and shaving the rest of his head. As well as the tea-plants which motivated the trip, he brought back chrysanthemums, azaleas, and now commonplace plants such as the wind-flower *(Anemone hupehensis)* and *Jasminium nudiflorum,* the winter-flowering jasmine. The important expeditions of Frank Ludlow and Major George Sherriff, between 1933 and 1949 were carried out with military precision – Sherriff had the forethought to sow vegetable seeds along the way to provide fresh food – and brought back the seed which helped to create places such as the late Bobby Masterton's garden at Cluny House, near Aberfeldy.

The thrill of discovery, the beauty of unexplored places – and some clue as to why anyone risks life for a plant clinging half- hidden to a mountainside – is found in the poetry of letters and notes left by the collectors who often died before they could indulge in the luxury of autobiography. Francis Masson (1741- 1805) an Aberdonian collecting for Kew in South Africa, witnessed a country 'enamalled with the greatest number of flowers I ever saw of exquisite beauty and fragrance'. But perhaps the opening up of China (and the enormous variety of plants packed into a vividly contrasting terrain) inspired the greatest excitement of all in collectors. 'In the morning', Forrest wrote, 'the sun as it touches the tops of the Mekong divide sends wide shafts of turquoise light down the side gullies to the river which seems to be transformed to silver.' Ludlow completed his last expedition in 1949 leaving the Tsangpo area of Tibet with great reluctance: 'Nature has run riot there. New species by the dozen flaunting their blooms asking for discovery and demanding a name'.

Many of the seeds sent home by Ludlow and Sherriff had already been introduced by Forrest – and many of Forrest's collections had been discovered by the nineteenth century

French missionaries such as Père Delavay and Abbé Soulie. Forrest first saw the plants of the Himalayas as dried specimens when he was herbarium assistant at the Royal Botanic Garden Edinburgh. Early explorers of the eighteenth century brought home live plants by sea in miniature glasshouses and few survived the long journey. Ludlow and Sherriff had the advantage of aeroplanes. But Forrest was remarkably successful in getting large quantities of viable seed back from the wild, training local people in Yunnan to gather seed from the plants he identified – on his last trip in 1932 he recorded 'Two mule loads of good clean seed, representing some 4- 5000 specimens. If all goes well I shall have made a rather glorious and satisfactory finish to all my past years of labour'. He died of a heart attack on a duck shooting trip before he could get home.

Forrest worked closely with the Royal Botanic Garden which always examined his botanical specimens and had a share of his seed. Behind every great collector is a sympathetic scientific assessor back home. 'There is a certain inevitability about the entry of really first class plants into cultivation' writes Alice Coats in *The Quest for Plants,* 'if one man does not bring them, another will – but gardeners probably owe more to the person who established a plant in cultivation than to its first discoverer.' So many of Forrest's rediscoveries pay tribute in their name to the missionaries, soldiers and surgeons who first found them but Forrest's seeds, like those of Ludlow and Sherriff, and the new generations of hardy collectors, gave birth to gardens.

Lathraea clandestina, *native to south west Europe, pictured flowering in early spring at the Royal Botanic Garden Edinburgh: a parasite often found on roots of willow and poplar trees and which, once established, can be detrimental to the host plant.*

THE PLANTSMAN'S GARDEN

The plants illustrated in these and the following pages all come from the Royal Botanic Garden Edinburgh.
Above: *the heath garden* ***Opposite:*** *Hordeum jubatum, 'Squirrel tail grass', an annual from North and South America and Siberia, closely related to barley, grown for the decorative feathery spike.*

THE PLANTSMAN'S GARDEN

Prunus x yedoensis, *introduced from Japan at the beginning of the century is widely planted as a street tree in Tokyo (Yedo or Edo being the old name of the city). A small tree with a spreading habit which makes a spectacular display of flowers, it is known as the Yoshino Cherry.*

THE PLANTSMAN'S GARDEN

Opposite: Tropaeolum speciosum, *the Chilean flame nasturtium, (mis-named the Scottish flame flower) a hardy climber usually seen brightening old yew hedges in west coast gardens, was brought back by William Lobb for Veitch nurseries in 1846. Scarlet flowers in summer are followed by brilliant blue fruits.*
Above: Clematis 'Bill MacKenzie', *a vigorous climber selected and named after Bill MacKenzie, curator of Chelsea Physic Garden. Thick petalled blooms are quickly followed by silky seed heads.*

Above left: Stellera chamaejasme, *extremely rare in cultivation, pictured displaying pink and white flowers at the Royal Botanic Garden Edinburgh. In Nepal vast numbers are seen bearing yellow flowers but in gardens it hardly ever sets seed.*
Above right: Kniphofia galpinii, *a decorative 'Red Hot Poker' which grows widely in the Transvaal, was introduced into gardens around fifty years ago and is highly valued as a late blooming herbaceous plant producing orange yellow flowers in September or October. **Below left:*** Synthyris stellata, *blooms early in March and April and is found wild in the Columbia Gorge, Washington and Oregon. It rarely exceeds eight inches in height but old established plants produce hundreds of Veronica-like flowers. **Below right:*** Allium amabile, *a dainty onion no more than six inches high, collected by George Forrest in 1922 in north west Yunnan. At one time known as* Allium yunnanensis. ***Opposite:*** Salix cascadensis, *showing pink-tinged male catkins, from west North America where it grows on the high alpine areas of the Cascade mountains.*

THE PLANTSMAN'S GARDEN

Opposite: Narcissus asturiensis *appears early enough to bloom through snow. Native to Spain and Portugal, it is really a miniature King Alfred daffodil, approximately two inches high.* **Above left:** Bulbocodium vernum, *a small spring-flowering bulb closely allied to the autumn-flowering* Colchicum, *native to central Europe where it grows in high meadows.* **Above right:** Omphalogramma souliei, *a member of the Primula family with large purple flowers was introduced into cultivation by George Forrest but the name commemorates Abbé Soulie a French Jesuit Missionary who discovered many plants in the same area.*

THE PLANTSMAN'S GARDEN

Opposite: Victoria amazonica, *showing underside of leaf, the intricate arrangement of thick and thin veins said to have inspired Paxton's design for the Crystal Palace. Originally named* Victoria regia *in honour of Queen Victoria, it is popularly known as the giant water lily. It has rose-coloured flowers up to twelve inches wide and leaves strong enough to support a child.* **Above:** Musa sanguinea, *one of the many species of banana native to Assam where it grows to around four feet. It is so named because of the blood red sheath surrounding the floral cluster. The developing fruit are the green bases to the yellow flowers.*

Above: Ananas comosus *'Variegatus'. The variegated form of the pineapple from Brazil grown as a decorative glasshouse plant.* **Left:** *Sarmienta repens, a creeping or climbing dwarf species from Chile, which will either form mats on the ground or ascend trees in moist warm forests and in greenhouses roots into staging tops.* **Right:** *Agapetes serpens originally introduced from Darjeeling, India about a century ago, has been a popular cool greenhouse plant for many years.*
Opposite: The fernhouse at the Royal Botanic Garden Edinburgh.

THE PLANTSMAN'S GARDEN

Opposite: species of Nomocharis, Meconopsis *and* Primula *found wild in north west China by Kingdon Ward and George Forrest are now naturalised in Cluny House gardens near Aberfeldy.* **Above left:** *candelabra primulas, hybrids between* P. beesiana *and* P. bulleyana *at Cluny – 'the plants of everybody' discovered by Forrest in a moist valley in the Lichiang range in 1906.* **Above right:** *Clematis macropetala, from Kansu in China, first recorded in 1742 but lost sight of until the turn of the century when it was rediscovered by Purdom and its seed was distributed by Farrer.*

THE PLANTSMAN'S GARDEN

Above: Primula kisoana, *the very unusual white form of a rare primula, a recent introduction from Japan where the pink form has been in cultivation for centuries.*
Opposite below: Primula whitei (P. bhutanica), *the blue-flowered plant, introduced into cultivation by Ludlow and Sherriff in 1936 by which time living plants could be flown home. In the corner is a white form of* Primula edgeworthii *named in honour of Michael Edgeworth of the East India Company and sent back by Winter in 1908.* **Opposite above:** Primula griffithii, *an extremely rare plant found 15,000 feet up in Bhutan by Ludlow and Sherriff on their last trip in 1949. Named in honour of William Griffith, a British botanist and doctor, who collected in India and Afghanistan in the last century.*

THE PLANTSMAN'S GARDEN

Opposite and below left: Lilium oxypetalum, *was first identified early in the last century. Sherriff collected the wild yellow form in 1939 in Haranghati. The purple form is known as* var. insigne. *Above left:* Lilium mackliniae. *Seed collected wild in Manipur by Frank Kingdon Ward in 1946 first flowered in cultivation in 1948, and is named after his wife who accompanied him on the expedition. Above right:* Trillium grandiflorum *'Flore pleno' showing the white double-flowered variety at Cluny. A collector's item, the wake robin is native to woods of eastern North America. Below right:* Trillium chloropetalum (T. sessile), *mottled foliage with white, pink, red or purple flowers, found in California a century ago.*

THE PLANTSMAN'S GARDEN

Nomocharis aperta, *above left*, discovered by Père Delavay and brought into cultivation by Forrest from Yunnan in 1928. Nomocharis pardanthina *above centre*, (nomocharis means grace of the pasture and pardanthina, spotted like a male panther), another Forrest and Delavay discovery which first flowered at Edinburgh's Royal Botanic Garden in 1914. The remaining pictures show the range of decoration as the plants hybridise at Cluny – they grow better in the cool conditions of Scottish gardens than anywhere else.

THE PLANTSMAN'S GARDEN

Opposite: a cosmopolitan border at Logan. Cordyline australis *(New Zealand) forms the background to* Kniphofia *(South Africa), white everlasting* Anaphalis *(N.East Asia) The trunk on the left is* Trachycarpus fortunei, *the Chusan palm from China, with the Chilean* Tropaeolum speciosum *on the wall behind.*
Above: Deschampsia caespitosa, *a tufted hair grass common throughout the British Isles, dominates a collection of grasses at Logan.*

THE PLANTSMAN'S GARDEN

The garden at Belhaven House was created by Sir George Taylor, Director of the Stanley Smith Horticultural Trust, who accompanied Ludlow and Sherriff on their 1938 Himalayan expedition. Although Belhaven is an alkaline garden, Sir George was determined to have some representation of choice calcifuge Himalayan plants (with which his name has been associated over the years.) This has been achieved by the use of troughs and peat beds. **Above left:** *the Trough Garden.*
Above right: *peat beds displaying a wide range of alpine rhododendrons.*
Below left: Clematis armandii, *shown here in its white form 'Snowdrift', is a native of China and one of the earliest flowering species.* **Below right:** Crocus vernus var. albiflorus *and* Erythronium tuolumnense. **Opposite:** *the early spring alpines* Primula marginata *and* Draba *brighten a corner of the Trough Garden.*

THE PLANTSMAN'S GARDEN

Above: a collection of Bonsai at Dundonnell displayed in the shade of lath-houses which provide the cool, moist conditions needed to prevent drying out.
Opposite: Chamaecyparis obtusa *from Japan, a forest tree which will grow to ninety feet.*

THE PLANTSMAN'S GARDEN

*Opposite: attractively dwarfed old pine grown in a lead container at Dundonnell. Moss indicates the moist environment. **Above:** Chamaecyparis, the Hinoki cypress introduced by Veitch in 1861 is a favourite Japanese subject for dwarfing. The twisted trunk indicates its old age.*

THE PLANTSMAN'S GARDEN

*Above: the heath garden at Threave. White heather surrounded by the yellow-leaved form of winter-flowering heath from the Alps.
Opposite: Scottish natives, purple thyme and white clover, carpet spaces between stepping stones through the scree at Threave.*

THE PLANTSMAN'S GARDEN

Above left: white rambling rose creeps over stone steps at Mellerstain House.
Above right: New Zealand daisy, Celmisia, blends with European flag iris at Leith Hall.
Opposite: a Scottish meadow at Inverewe. Marguerites, dandelions and hawkweed.

LIST OF GARDENS AND INDEX

The following list gives ownership and outline details of access to all properties illustrated in this book, cross-referenced to page numbers. Further details of gardens to visit in Scotland are to be found in **Scotland's Gardens**, the guide to gardens open under Scotland's Gardens Scheme.

Royal Botanic Garden Edinburgh
Inverleith Row, Edinburgh
Open all year (except Christmas Day and New Years Day) pages 14-15, 31, 62-63, 90-91, 126, 128, 129, 130-143

Achamore House (Mr & Mrs D Holt)
Ardminish, Isle of Gigha
Open all year
pages 12, 13, 15, 31, 62

Ardtornish House (Mrs F Raven)
Lochaline, Morvern, Argyll
Open April-October
pages 15, 18-19

Bargany House
(Mr J Dalrymple-Hamilton)
Old Daily, Ayrshire
Open March-October
page 50

Barncluith House (Mr & Mrs J O Graham)
Hamilton, Lanarkshire
No public access
pages 32, 64-65

Belhaven House
No public access
pages 154-155

Benmore
See Younger Botanic Garden

Blair Castle (The Duke of Atholl)
Blair Atholl, Perthshire
Open April-October
pages 14, 29, 32

Brodick Castle (The National Trust for Scotland)
Brodick, Isle of Arran
Open all year
pages 31, 56-57, 87

Carnell (Mr & Mrs J R Findlay and Mr J Findlay)
Hurlford, Ayrshire
Open on special dates only under Scotland's Gardens Scheme or by appointment
pages 10, 112-113

Castle of Mey
(H.M. Queen Elizabeth the Queen Mother)
Mey, Caithness
Open on special dates only under Scotland's Gardens Scheme
page 104

Cawdor Castle (The Countess Cawdor)
Cawdor, Nairnshire
Open May-October
pages 66, 116

Cluny House (Mr J & Mrs W Mattingley)
Aberfeldy, Perthshire
Open March-October
pages 10, 127, 128, 144-151

Crarae Glen Garden
(Crarae Gardens Charitable Trust)
Minard, by Inveraray, Argyll
Open all year
pages 8, 15, 25, 30, 31, 33, 38-41, 52-53, 61

Crathes Castle (The National Trust for Scotland)
Banchory, Kincardineshire
Open all year
pages 28, 70, 83, 117

Dalkeith Park (Buccleuch Estates Ltd)
Dalkeith, Midlothian
Open April-October
pages 70, 88-89

Dawyck Botanic Garden
(Royal Botanic Garden Edinburgh)
Stobo, nr Peebles, Peeblesshire
Open March-October
pages 9, 15, 31, 46, 58, 84

LIST OF GARDENS AND INDEX

Drummond Castle
(The Grimsthorpe and Drummond Castle Trust)
Muthill, Pershire
Open May-October
pages 13, 14, 26-27, 92, 119

Dundee University Botanic Garden
(University of Dundee)
Perth Road, Dundee, Angus
Open all year
page 54

Dundonnell (Mr A Roger & Mr N Roger)
By Little Loch Broom, Ross and Cromarty
Open on special dates only under Scotland's
Gardens Scheme or by special arrangement
pages 9, 55, 92, 156-159

Dunmore Pineapple
(The National Trust for Scotland)
Airth, Stirlingshire
Open by arrangement with the Landmark Trust
pages 84, 85

Dunrobin Castle (The Sutherland Trust)
Golspie, Sutherland
Open March-October
pages 13, 28, 115

Duns Castle Nature Reserve
(Scottish Wildlife Trust)
Duns, Berwickshire
Open all year
page 47

Earlshall Castle
(The Baron & Baroness of Earlshall)
Leuchars, Fife
Open by appointment only
pages 67, 68, 70, 78-79, 109, 122-123

Edzell Castle
(Historic Scotland)
Edzell, Angus
Open all year
page 111

Falkland Palace (The National Trust of Scotland)
Falkland, Fife
Open April-October
pages 68, 70, 72-74

Fingask Castle (Mr & Mrs Murray Threipland)
No public access
pages 94-97, 118

Glamis Castle Italian Garden
(The Earl of Strathmore and Kinghorne;
Strathmore Estates (Holding) Ltd)
Glamis, Forfar, Angus
Open April-October
page 114

Glasgow Botanic Garden
(Glasgow City Council)
Great Western Road, Glasgow
Open all year
pages 92-93

Haddo House (The National Trust for Scotland)
Tarves, Aberdeenshire
Open all year
page 99

Inverewe (The National Trust for Scotland)
Poolewe, Ross and Cromarty
Open all year
pages 15, 21, 31, 32, 51, 163

Kailzie (Lady Angela Buchan-Hepburn)
By Peebles, Peeblesshire
Open all year
page 105

Keir (His Excellency Mahdi Al-Tajir)
Dunblane, Perthshire
No public access
pages 31, 33, 42-45, 55, 59, 107

Kellie Castle (The National Trust for Scotland)
Pittenweem, Fife
Open all year
pages 67, 68, 70, 75-77, 84, 99, 110

Kildrummy Castle
(Kildrummy Castle Garden Trust)
Kildrummy, Alford, Aberdeenshire
Open April-October
page 48

LIST OF GARDENS AND INDEX

Kinross House (Sir David Montgomery Bt)
Kinross, Kinross-shire
Open May-September
pages 13, 14, 28, 98

Leith Hall (The National Trust for Scotland)
Kennethmont, Aberdeenshire
Open all year
pages 84, 162

Logan Botanic Garden
(Royal Botanic Garden Edinburgh)
Port Logan, by Stranraer, Wigtownshire
Open March-October
pages 9, 15, 20, 106, 117, 152-153

Malleny House (The National Trust for Scotland)
Balerno, Midlothian
Open all year
pages 71, 80, 114

Megginch Castle
(Captain Drummond of Megginch & Baroness Strange)
Errol, Pertshire
Open April-Juiy, September-October (Wednesday pm only); August (daily)
pages 81, 82, 120-121

Mellerstain House (The Earl of Haddington)
Gordon, Berwickshire
Open May-September (not Saturdays)
pages 87, 162

Mertoun (The Duke of Sutherland)
St Boswells, Roxburghshire
Open April-September (Saturdays, Sundays and Monday Public Holidays)
pages 83, 114

Monteviot (The Earl and Countess of Ancram)
Jedburgh, Roxburghshire
Open on special dates only under Scotland's Gardens Scheme
pages 14, 15, 22-23, 68

Pitmedden (The National Trust for Scotland)
Pitmedden, Aberdeenshire
Open May-October
pages 69, 99, 108, 114, 124-125

Priorwood (The National Trust for Scotland)
Melrose, Roxburghshire
Open April-December
page 110

St Andrews Botanic Garden
(Fife Council)
St Andrews, Fife
Open April-October; November-March (weekdays)
page 54

Saltoun Hall (Proprietors of Saltoun Hall)
Pencaitland, East Lothian
No public access
page 86

Stobhall (The Earl and Countess of Perth)
By Perth, Perthshire
Open on special dates only under Scotland's Gardens Scheme
pages 9, 24, 68, 99

Stobo Water Garden
(Mr H Seymour and Mr C Seymour)
Stobo, Peeblesshire
Open by appointment and on special dates only under Scotland's Gardens Scheme
pages 48, 49

Strone House Garden and Pinetum
(Cairndow Estates)
Cairndow, Argyll
Open April-October
page 60

Threave (The National Trust for Scotland)
Castle Douglas, Kirkcudbrightshire
Open all year
pages 160-161

Torosay Castle (Mr Christopher James)
Craignure, Isle of Mull
Open all year
pages 9, 10, 11, 14, 16-17, 69, 100-103

Younger Botanic Garden
(Royal Botanic Garden Edinburgh)
Benmore, by Dunoon, Argyll
Open March-October
pages 15, 32, 33, 34-37

Dr Brinsley Burbidge, a graduate of St Andrews and Edinburgh, was until 1986 employed as Principal Scientific Officer at the Royal Botanic Garden Edinburgh.

An enthusiastic traveller and plant collector, he has always allied these pursuits to his great passion for photography. His explorations have taken him from Soviet Central Asia, Siberia, and the Western Himalaya to East Africa, the Andes and Hawaii, as well as leading plant study tours of Greece and the Caucasus.

He is a Fellow of the Royal Photographic Society, a member of its Distinction Panel, and sits on the Royal Horticultural Society's Picture Committee.

Dr Burbidge is now Head of Information and Exhibitions Division at the Royal Botanic Gardens, Kew.

Fay Young is a freelance journalist living in Edinburgh. She is a contributor to the *Guardian*, *Observer* and *Scotsman* and also writes a regular column for *Insider*, Scotland's leading business magazine.

A keen gardener and allotment holder, she is married and has three sons.